L Is for Loving

An ABC For the Way You Feel

For my grandmother
Eleanor Pike

K.W.-M.

For information address Hyperion Books for Children,
114 Fifth Avenue, New York, New York 10011-5690.

First Edition

1 3 5 7 9 10 8 6 4 2

Library of Congress Cataloging-in-Publication Data

Wilson-Max, Ken.
L is for Loving: an ABC for the way you feel/
by Ken Wilson-Max. – 1st ed. p. cm.
Summary: An alphabet book presenting the range
of emotions that we may feel, from angelic to zippy.
ISBN 0-7868-0527-7 (trade ed.) – ISBN 0-7868-2460-3 (lib. bdg.)
1. Emotions in children – Juvenile literature.
2. English language – Alphabet – Juvenile literature.
[1. Emotions. 2. Alphabet.] I. Title.
BF723.E6W57 1999 152.4 – dc21
[E] 98-54703 CIP AC

L Is for Loving

An ABC for the Way You Feel

Ken Wilson-Max

Hyperion
Books for Children
New York

A a

Angelic

Angelic is how I feel when Mommy
tells me I have been a good boy.

B b

Brave

Going to the doctor can be a little scary, so you have to be brave.

C c Cuddly

My teddy is cuddly,
warm, and totally lovable.

Dd Dizzy

Spinning around and
around makes me dizzy.

Ee Exhausted

When I spin too much, it wears me out. Now I am exhausted!

Ff

Friendly

We like to play together
and be friendly.

G g

Greedy

Ice cream makes me greedy.
I always eat too much of it.

H h

Happy

I feel so happy,
I cannot stop smiling.

I i

Innocent

When Daddy asked me if
I had drawn on the wall,
I tried to look very innocent.

J j

Jealous

My friend got a bigger toy car than me. It made me jealous.

K k   Kind

Being friends with someone
means that you are kind to them.

L l

Loving

We are a loving family.

M m

Miserable

It was too wet outside to take my dog
for a walk. It made us both miserable.

N n

Noisy

Sometimes my friends and
I like to be loud and noisy.

Oo

When I dress up and
pretend I'm a star,
I feel outrageous.

Outrageous

P p

Proud

We are proud of our accomplishments.

Q q

Quiet

Today I feel quiet . . .
ssshhhhh!

R r Responsible

Every day I have to remember to feed my cat. That makes me responsible.

S s

Silly

If I feel like being silly,
I make funny faces . . . all day!

T t

Tired

At the end of the day, I feel tired.

Uu

Upset

Sometimes bad things happen
that make me upset inside.

V v

Vocal

When we sing together
we feel vocal!

Ww Worried

I was worried when Daddy was not feeling well, so I made him a special card.

Get Well Soon!
I love you Daddy
x x x

X x xx (I love you)

He was so happy when he got it that he gave me a big hug and kiss. I love my daddy.

Y y

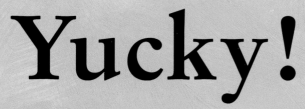

My little brother threw his dinner all over me!
I felt so yucky that I had to change my clothes.

Z z

Zippy

Today I am feeling
zippy–watch me go!